HAND PAINTED PORCELAIN

The Australasian Porcelain Art Teachers'
Collection
1991

Margaret Dixon

HAND PAINTED PORCELAIN

The Australasian Porcelain Art Teachers'
Collection
1991

Australasian Porcelain Art Teachers Inc.

(NSW Region)

ACKNOWLEDGMENTS

We gratefully acknowledge the time and effort of the 1989–1991 Australasian Executive and the members of the NSW Region in convening this Exhibition.

- Tricia Bradford, Australasian Chairman, and her Committee for compiling this pictorial report.
- Mr Michael Doulton, Company Ambassador, Royal Doulton.
- Hilda Bloxham, Photography where required.
- Barbara Torkington, Illustration.
- All of those who supported this enormous exercise with financial assistance, time and expertise.
- All exhibitors
- Australasian Executive
  Tricia Bradford—Chairman
  Fay Robinson—Vice Chairman
  Annette Strong—Secretary
  Pat Try—Treasurer
- Exhibition convenors—Brenda Matthews and Audrey Pines
- Pictorial Report Convenor—Lilian Beer

Front cover: Jan Kellaway
Back cover: Fay Robinson—'Crock Ness Monster'

© Australasian Porcelain Art Teachers Inc. 1992

Published on behalf of
Australasian Porcelain Art Teachers Inc.
in 1992 by Kangaroo Press Pty Ltd
3 Whitehall Road (P.O. Box 75) Kenthurst NSW 2156
Typeset by G.T. Setters Pty Limited
Printed in Hong Kong through Colorcraft Ltd

ISBN 0 86417 443 8

Contents

Introduction 6

Foreword 7

Award Winning Entries 8

New South Wales 11

Queensland 55

Western Australia 63

Tasmania 69

Victoria 77

South Australia 97

New Zealand 111

Venezuela 125

USA 126

Germany 129

Brazil 130

Malaysia 131

Singapore 132

Japan 133

Switzerland 141

'The Last Word' 143

Index 144

Introduction

It is with pleasure and pride I present to you the work of porcelain artists who exhibited at the 1991 biennial exhibition in Sydney.

The skill and talent required to produce these works of art and heirlooms of the future is obvious; this record of handpainted porcelain will provide a historical report of the impressive and wide variety of traditional and modern techniques used in today's contemporary art world.

Sadly, not all the artists who exhibited are represented here and this is our loss. We acknowledge their work in its absence along with the featured artists.

Tricia Bradford
Australasian Chairman 1989–1991
Australasian Porcelain Art Teachers Inc.

Foreword

It was with great pleasure that I accepted the invitation to open the 1991 Australasian Porcelain Art Teachers' Association Exhibition. At Royal Doulton we value the special skills of our ceramic artists and I always enjoy seeing these talents being celebrated in such a positive and exciting display.

In five generations of china making, Royal Doulton has evolved from a small family pottery to become the world's leading manufacturer of fine bone china. In that time we have seen technological advances which have revolutionised our industry and yet we have never found a machine which can compete with an artist. Our products are sought after by collectors worldwide, often because of the human component in their manufacture, and it is the artist's contribution which distinguishes these pieces as works of art.

The quality of the artists' work at this exhibition was truly world class, as was the range of styles and techniques on display. I commend to you this pictorial record of a most impressive occasion, and I look forward to viewing further exhibitions on future trips to Australia.

Michael Doulton
Company Ambassador
Royal Doulton China

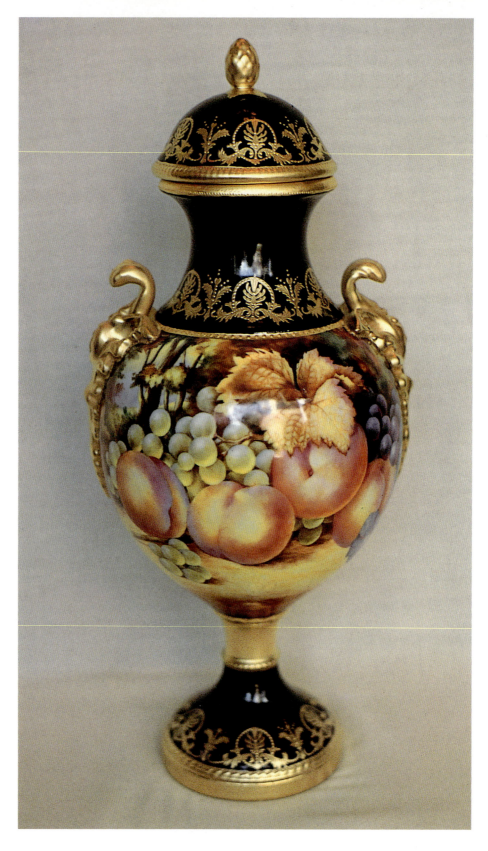

Louise Hopping (NSW)

Winner
Teaching Institute of Porcelain Art (NSW)
Popular Choice Award

Brenda Henderson (WA)

Winner
Isobel Marshall Agnew Trophy
for
Most Original and Creative Design on a Commercial Piece of Porcelain

Barbara Dimitri (NSW)

Winner
Ellen Massey Porcelain Fine Art Award
for
A Display of Excellence

NEW SOUTH WALES

Winner
Bank of New Zealand Trophy
Awarded to the APAT Region
exhibiting the most original and creative works of art

Wildflower urn

Jan Kellaway

White azaleas
on bone china

Runner up—Popular choice prize

Louise Hopping

Barbara Dimitri

Sandra Brown
'Rainbow serpent dreaming'
35 cm plate

Tricia Bradford
'Fragile environment'
5 cm glass ball fired onto lustre
and gold dipped design

Sandra Brown
'Pupunyah Dreaming'
Round trinket box 15 cm diameter

Tricia Bradford
'Salvation'
Framed 30 cm tile

Marjorie Roche
'Musk lorikeets'
25 cm plaque

Marjorie Roche
'Ringtail possum'
15 × 11 cm oval plaque,
supported on carved
bush timber base

Joan Curtis
'Seascape'

**Joan Curtis

'Australia Gold'
32.5 cm plaque

Barbara Adams

Contemporary vase
Glass chipping, lustre and texture paste

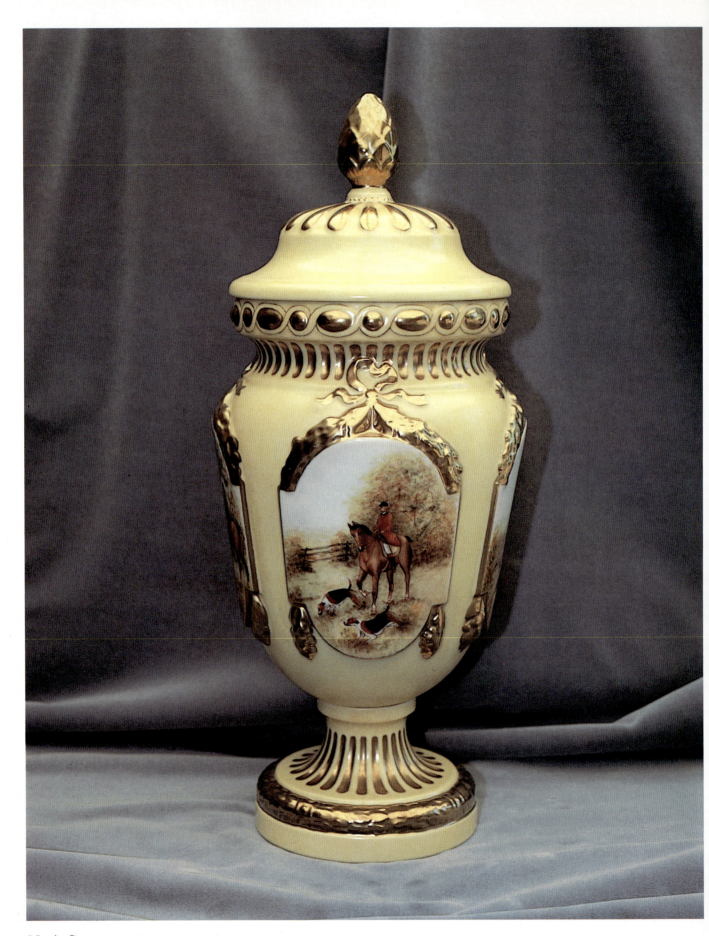

Mavis Carter
'English hunting scene'

Mavis Carter
'Fishing Village in Milano'
47.5 cm

Jean Spokes
'Rose and Tumble'

'My favourite parrot'

Trixie Emery

'Banjo Upton'

'His Domain'
25 cm plate
Falcon with special effects background

Dorothy Prest

'Pals'
25 cm plate
Dingoes—etched look border

Marion Goard
'Wanderland, Fitzroy Falls'
Umbrella stand

Fay Green
30 cm plate
Stylised poppies
Multicoloured lustres

Erica Harrison
Teaset

Shirley Hanbury
Rose urn

Shirley Hanbury
Floral rabbits

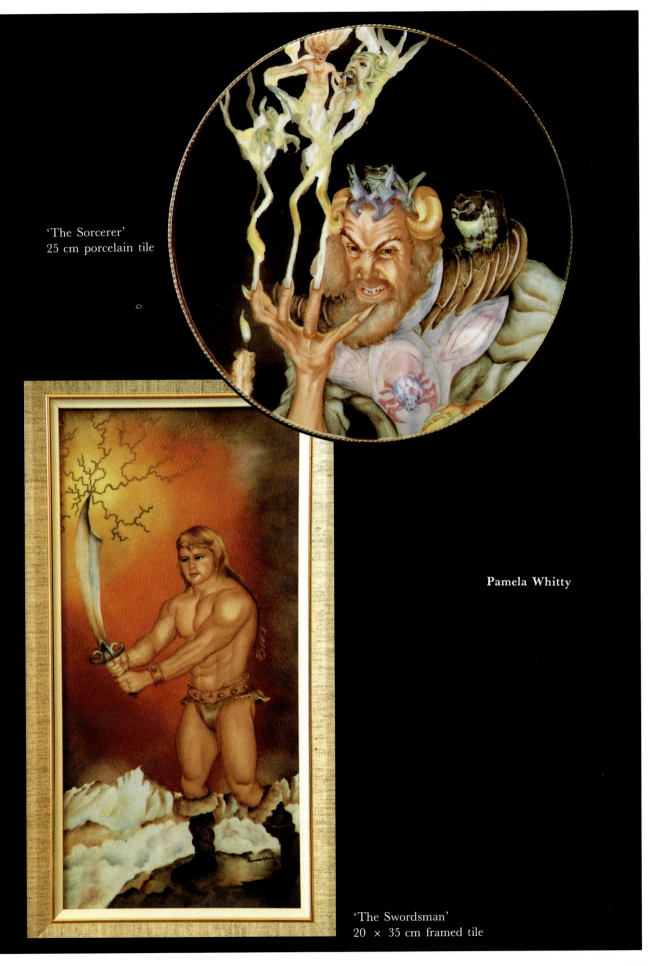

'The Sorcerer'
25 cm porcelain tile

Pamela Whitty

'The Swordsman'
20 × 35 cm framed tile

Lorraine Pratley
'Fishscaling'

Marion Goard
'Theatre'
Framed montage
Experimental section

Tile in pointillism

Heather Kiely

'Australia Dream'

Barbara Loader

Gwen MacFarlane
'Gang Gang Cockatoos'

'Peacock in Plum Tree'

Beth Rowe

'Playful Koalas'

Lorna Mitchell

Daphne McKinnon
'Springtime'
27.5 cm vase

Deirdre Marlborough

Audrey Pines

Lynette Larkin

Del Lloyd
Small bone china pansy bowl

Abstract vase
Raised enamel, penwork, gold, lustre and metallic

Megan Campbell

Slumped glass bowl lustred and gilded
Experimental section

Chris Riley
'Ingrid Bergman'

Fay Robinson
'Porpoiseful'

Portrait on 30 cm round tile, set into silk frame
Appliquéed silk border

Di Curtin

'Fairy Lamp'
Porcelain base, handpainted silk shade

Hunting scene
30 cm sandwich tray

Val Johnson

Hunting scene
30 cm porcelain platter

Edith Saunders
35 cm azalea vase

Jenny Seccombe
'Flannel Flowers'
22.5 cm vase
Grounding, penwork and paint

Annette Seaman
'Old Man Roo'
Back and front of 17.5 cm vase

42

Lilian Beer
'Koala'
25 × 13 cm framed porcelain slab

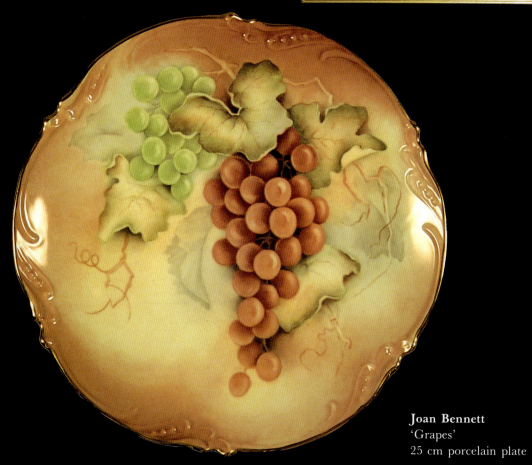

Joan Bennett
'Grapes'
25 cm porcelain plate

'Down a Dreamy Path'
22.5 cm pillow vase

Annette Strong

'Falling Fuchsias'
22.5 cm vase

44

Joyce Tarry

Glad Williams
'Sheep and Stream'

Barbara Torkington

Barbara Torkington

46

33.75 cm tray

Ena Wallace

25 cm porcelain vase with cavity

Pat Try
'Stained Glass Window'
Frame handcarved from Australian red cedar

'Aboriginal Girl'
Stand from the root of an
Australian silky oak

Pat Try

'Common Ringtailed
Possum'
Framed, copper lustre, acid etching

49

Lexie Watt
'Aboriginal girl and dingo'

Lexie Watt
'Faerie tile'
with leadlight dragon frame

'White Roses'
35 cm urn
Metallic ground

Margaret Towler

'Country Garden'
30 cm pitcher and bowl

52

Karen Carter
'Summer Garden'

Margaret Towler
'Tea for Two'
Miniature bisque teaset

'Old Salt'
Sepia tones

Jan Gowan

'Australian Elegance'
Australian wildflowers—European style

QUEENSLAND

Una Edwards
'Orchids—*Cymbidium balkis* × *Earlyana*'

Jean Harris
Limoges jewellery box

Maureen Laverty
30 cm iris vase

Georgina Gould
'Greek husband and wife'
3rd place popular choice award

'I think, by the expressions on their faces, this couple enjoys very loving and happy companionship'

Georgina Gould

'Popov, the Russian Clown'
30 cm porcelain plate

Patricia Robertson

'Ducks'

'Unicorn After Morning Swim'
Bone china urn

Vera Canale

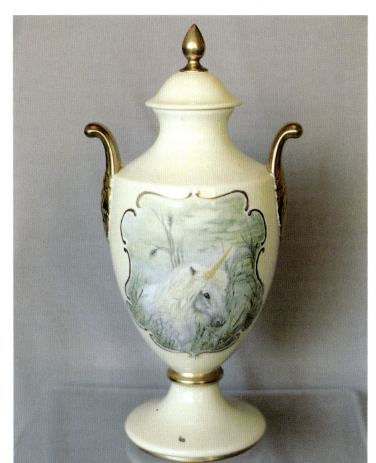

Lakeland scene
Antique gold with burnished gold trim

61

Shirley Bailey
'Cartoon'
Two 25 × 20 cm porcelain slabs framed as book

WESTERN AUSTRALIA

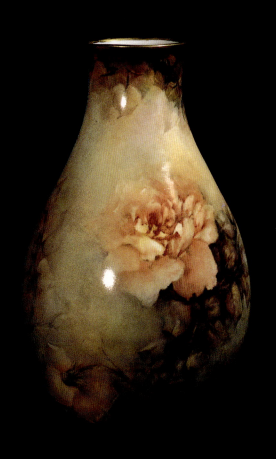

'Only a Rose'

June Laird

Contemporary vase, sand grounded

Leschenaultia vase

Joy Crowe

'Blackboys'

Brenda Henderson
Legend on back of plate:
'Design based on the Kimberley-WA Bungle Bungle National Park.
Around 3000 sq. m and 350 million years old—extremely fragile.
The striped rock has thin outer skins of black lichen and orange
silica—when broken exposes soft sandstone. Far Palms cling to the cliffs.'

Brenda Henderson

Gloria Paxman
'Music from Melkor'

TASMANIA

'Bushfire'
Textured tree trunks and enamel fire

Wendy Burbury

'Peace Rose with Dewdrop'

'Stag'
25 cm bone china plate

Elaine Howell

Bone china loving cup
Front and back views

Gwynneth Dunham
Antique oval dish
European design

Pat Moore
Fruit plate
Wedgwood bone china

'Rottweiler'

Arleen Spencer

'Cradle Mountain, Tasmania'

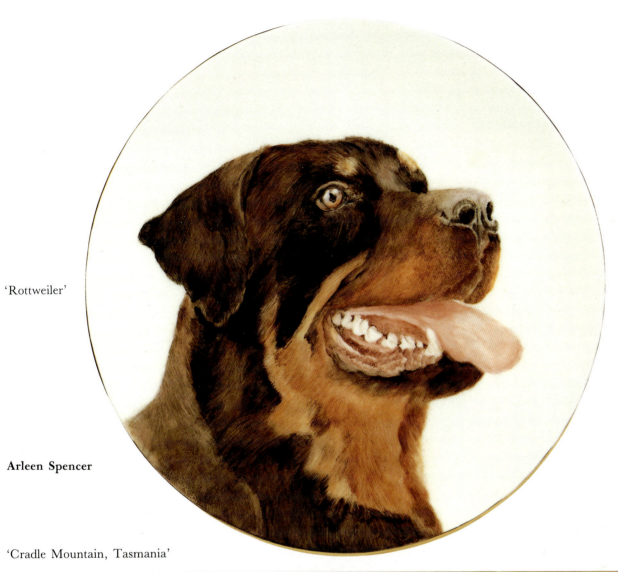

Jean Murrell
35 cm bone china urn

Jean Murrell
32.5 cm framed tile

Marilyn Sampson
'Red Roses'
Italian matt floor tile

Gwynneth Walker
'Birds'
24 cm pillow vase

VICTORIA

Aboriginal Dreamtime story:
'How the swans had black feathers'

Joyce Austin

'Wildflowers'
25 cm bone china plate

78

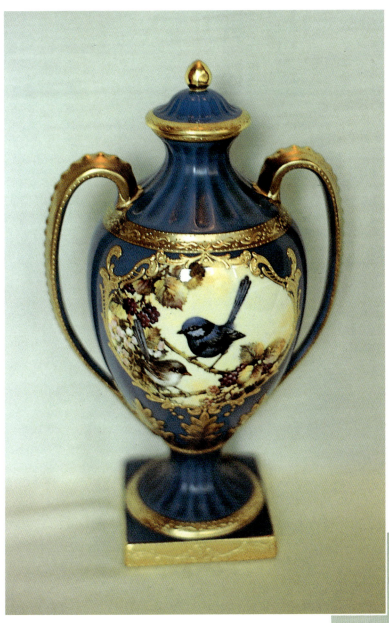

Jo Armstrong
Spode bone china urn

Back view

Heather Boucher

Silvana Careri
'Pink Roses'
30 cm plate

Win Carter
'Pink Blush'

Win Carter

Valma Crerar
'Cape Ricardo'

Jenifer Davies
Fruit bowl

Evelyn Hales
'Waratahs and Flannel Flowers'
25 cm bowl

Genevieve Hanley
'Sunrise Across the River'

Helen Dundon

84

Helen Dundon

Robyn Maddock

Robyn Maddock
30 cm Japanese porcelain tray

Joy Learmonth

Shirley Livingstone
20 cm bone china bowl

Raie Grenda
Australian natives floral plate

Lorraine Hansen
Painted and dusted grapes
30 cm German plate

36 cm urn

Valerie Macpherson

Dresden ruby roses
25 cm plate

Patsy Meldrum
60 cm floor plate
Painted from flowers photographed in Launceston, Tasmania

Patricia Redman
14 cm oval lidded canister

Judy Seymour
'Pheasants'
37.5 cm platter

Judy Seymour

Pauline Shinkfield

Margaret Smith
35 cm oval bone china platter

Anice Van Os
Hydrangea plate

Bette Tait
'Stag'—Scottish scene
17.5 cm bone china plate

Moira Treacher
'Coastal Banksia'—A mood painting

Valerie Bingley
37.5 cm urn

Lorraine Lucy

SOUTH AUSTRALIA

Beryl Bailey
'Friendship'

Margaret Faulks

Pat Brown

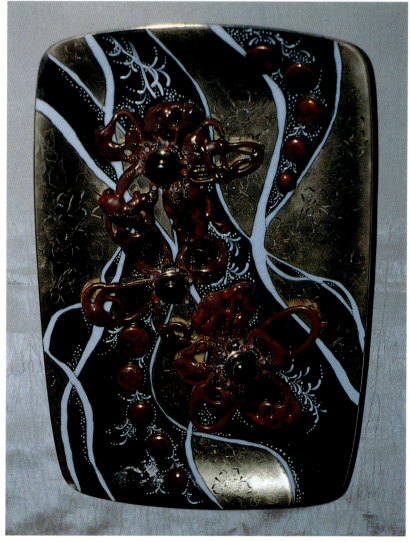

Margaret Faulks
Experimental exhibit

Beverley Ambridge
15 cm vase
Double cast porcelain, carved in greenware from white back to pink slip

100

Beverley Ambridge
37.5 cm porcelain thrown platter carved in greenware, part glazed and china painted

'Portrait of King Tutankhamen'

Margaret Box

'Death Mask of King Tutankhamen'

'Jessie and Jack'
Porcelain tiles 30 × 35 cm
Framed as one

Barbara Blackburn

'Herbert'
Porcelain tile, framed size 30 × 45 cm

Margaret Dixon
'Mottlecah'
30 cm plate

Margaret Dixon
'Mottlecah'

Lee Sanders

Ruth Seager
Formal arrangement

106

30 cm plate

Joyleen Grund

30 cm plate

107

Maureen Uzzell

Kirsten Christensen

Josie Robinson

Jean Stuchbery
'Historical Urn'
43 cm

109

Betty Hermel

NEW ZEALAND

Gay Carroll
25 cm green and gold penwork plate

Betty Sievers
'Rooster and Hen'
Lustred background

112

Pamela Comins
'Evolution'
25 cm vase, ground laid and texture

Denise Montgomery
'Fish, Crabs and Shells'

113

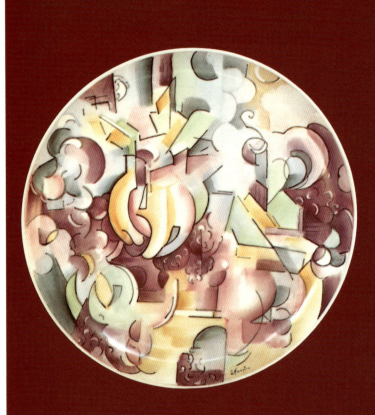

Shirley Hampton
Contemporary fruit

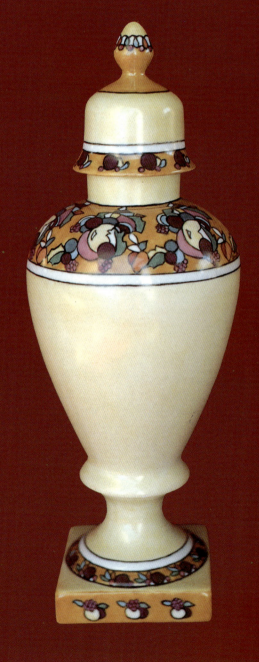

Shirley Hampton

'Grecian Scene'
30 cm dark blue ground vase

Valmai Hart-McEwan

'Portrait of a Young Girl'

115

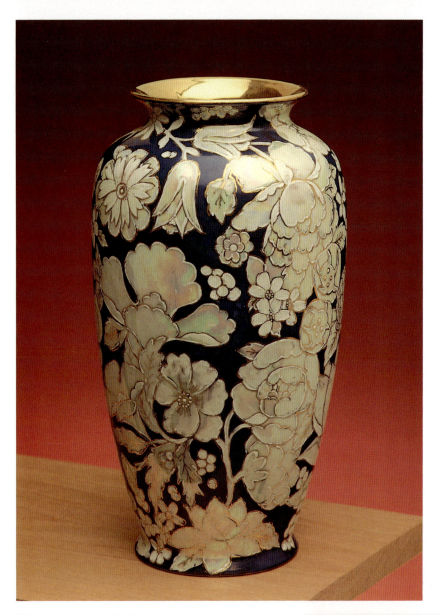

Blue ground classic 25 cm vase
Stylised flowers with mother-of-pearl lustre

Pamela Hobbs

Dresden design cutout bowl

116

Ona Kibby
'Fighting Cock'

Gwenda King
'Bush Landscape'
25 cm plate

Merle Loomans
'Sydney Sails'
Air blown lustre, metallics, texture and glass

Gwenda King
Landscape with textured grass and trees
Lustre, metallics, texture, and glass with chipping

Vivienne Mackintosh

Rosemary Crossley

Margaret Reed

120

Pamela Robertson
25 cm plate ground laid in ice blue with agate-etched gold band

Pamela Robertson

Grace Rodger
'Gate Scene'

Kathleen Saward
'Highland Cattle'

122

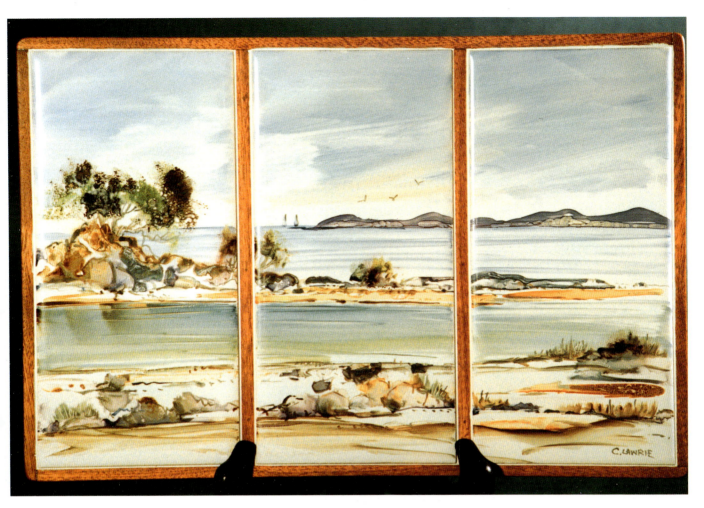

Cherry Lawrie
Triptych
Lustred landscape

Lyn Johnstone
'Body, Soul and Spirit'
Framed multimedia

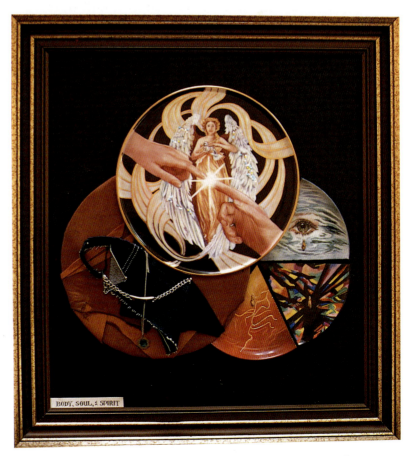

123

'Mum and I'
40 cm oval platter

Lyn Johnstone

'Janet's Garden'
35 cm vase

VENEZUELA

Relly Molinari

USA

Mary Ellen Haggerty Richards

Barbara Walker

Ruth Yatchman

Mary Patusky

GERMANY

Ursula Liebl

Ursula Liebl

BRAZIL

Carlos Spina

Rose Borges

MALAYSIA

'Fuchsias'

Sylvia Nobes

'Fuchsias'

SINGAPORE

Margaret Chew

JAPAN

Yumiko Okamura
Flowers

Bird and flowers

Yumiko Okamura

Bird and flowers

134

Fumi Ishido
'Flowering in Summer'

Hiroko Nagayama
'Farm Scene'

Birds

Kae Takeuchi

Bouquet

Akemi Aida

Nobuko Sasamoto
Christmas box

Bisque plate

Yumiko Fukuyo

Bisque plate

138

Yukie Hirano
Plate and decanter

Kayoko Sato
'My dogs'

SWITZERLAND

Ursula Polla

Hennie Fiedler

The Last Word

(for this book)

This pictorial exposition of the works exhibited at the Australasian Porcelain Art Teachers Exhibition and Convention held in Sydney in September 1991 serves as an authoritative guide to the artistry and craftsmanship practised by porcelain artists during the late part of the twentieth century. What a wonderful and dramatically interesting time we paint in!

For many years painting on porcelain remained a disciplined and structured art. Today's freedom of expression allows us to escape the set boundaries and expand on the techniques and presentation of the china to introduce exciting new concepts and interpretations of the existing traditions.

Viewers of such an exhibition as this may now appreciate the many and varied techniques which are used to enhance the pristine porcelain surface. Traditional and elegant art pieces contrasted sharply with modern styles. The regal deer maintained his royal position among the gilded and raised paste borders while contemporary platters and tiles enhanced by wooden frames, leadlight and silken borders introduced a refreshing new look to the display.

It is interesting to note that the pieces voted most popular by the general public and the majority of porcelain artists were traditional in both design and concept. The presentation of the second most popular choice was also traditional, although in these pieces the native floral arrangements were executed with a contemporary freedom of design and flair for movement.

Porcelain art is evolving at an ever increasing rate and its amalgamation with other mediums will only lead to continuous expansion of our knowledge and awareness as artists.

Another trend which was obvious was the pride and loyalty which the majority of artists appeared to have for their country. Native flora and fauna featured predominantly and it was the depiction of some of Australia's most rugged country which caught the imagination of the judges.

Our grateful thanks to all artists who participated in this memorable exhibition and to all those many people without whose assistance we would not have had the success we did.

Sincerely,

Tricia Bradford

Index

Adams, Barbara, NSW, 19
Aida, Akemi, Japan, 137
Ambridge, Beverley, SA, 100, 101
Armstrong, Jo, Vic, 79
Austin, Joyce, Vic, 78

Bailey, Beryl, SA, 98
Bailey, Shirley, Qld, 62
Beer, Lilian, NSW, 43
Bennett, Joan, NSW, 43
Bingley, Valerie, Vic, 95
Blackburn, Barbara, SA, 103
Borges, Rose, Brazil, 130
Boucher, Helen, Vic, 80
Box, Margaret, SA, 102
Bradford, Tricia, ACT, 15, 16
Brown, Pat, SA, 99
Brown, Sandra, NSW, 14, 15
Burbury, Wendy, Tas, 70

Campbell, Megan, NSW, 36
Canale, Vera, Qld, 61
Careri, Silvana, Vic, 80
Carroll, Gay, NZ, 112
Carter, Karen, ACT, 53
Carter, Mavis, NSW, 20, 21
Carter, Win, Vic, 81
Chew, Margaret, Singapore, 132
Christensen, Kirsten, SA, 108
Comins, Pamela, NZ, 113
Crerar, Valma, Vic, 82
Crossley, Rosemary, NZ, 119
Crowe, Joy, WA, 65
Curtin, Diane (Di), NSW, 39
Curtis, Joan, NSW, 18

Davies, Jenifer, Vic, 82
Dimitri, Barbara, NSW, 10, 13
Dixon, Margaret, SA, 2, 104, 105
Dundon, Helen, Vic, 84, 85
Dunham, Gwynneth, Tas, 72

Edwards, Una, Qld, 56
Emery, Trixie, NSW, 23

Faulks, Margaret, SA, 98, 99
Fiedler, Hennie, Switzerland, 142
Fukuyo, Yumiko, Japan, 138

Goard, Marion, NSW, 25, 28
Gould, Georgina, Qld, 58, 59
Gowan, Jan, NSW, 54
Green, Faye, NSW, 25
Grenda, Raie, Vic, 87
Grund, Joyleen, SA, 107

Hales, Evelyn, Vic, 83

Hampton, Shirley, NZ, 114
Hanbury, Shirley, NSW, 26
Hanley, Genevieve, Vic, 84
Hansen, Lorraine, Vic, 87
Harris, Jean, Qld, 57
Harrison, Erica, NSW, 26
Hart-McEwan, Valmai, NZ, 115
Hermel, Betty, SA, 110
Henderson, Brenda, WA, 9, 66, 67
Hirano, Yukie, Japan, 139
Hobbs, Pamela, NZ, 116
Hopping, Louise, NSW, 8, 13
Howell, Elaine, Tas, 71

Ishido, Fumi, Japan, 135

Johnson, Val, NSW, 40
Johnstone, Lyn, NZ, 123, 124

Kellaway, Jan, NSW, front cover, 12
Kibby, Ona, NZ, 117
Kiely, Heather, NSW, 29
King, Gwenda, NZ, 117, 118

Laird, June, WA, 64
Larkin, Lynette, NSW, 35
Laverty, Maureen, Qld, 57
Lawry, Cherry, NZ, 123
Learmonth, Joy, Vic, 86
Liebl, Ursula, Germany, 129
Livingstone, Shirley, Vic, 86
Lloyd, Del, NSW, 35
Loader, Barbara, NSW, 30
Loomans, Merle, NZ, 118
Lucy, Lorraine, Vic, 96

MacFarlane, Gwen, NSW, 30
Mackintosh, Vivienne, NZ, 119
Macpherson, Valerie, Vic, 88
Maddock, Robyn, Vic, 85
Marlborough, Deirdre, NSW, 33
McKinnon, Daphne, NSW, 33
Meldrum, Patricia (Patsy), Vic, 89
Mitchell, Lorna, NSW, 32
Molinari, Relly, Venezuela, 125
Montgomery, Denise, NZ, 113
Moore, Pat, Tas, 72
Murrell, Jean, Tas, 74, 75

Nagayama, Hiroko, Japan, 135
Nobes, Sylvia, Malaysia, 131

Okamura, Yumiko, Japan, 133, 134

Patusky, Mary, USA, 128
Paxman, Gloria, WA, 68
Pines, Audrey, NSW, 34

Polla, Ursula, Switzerland, 141
Pratley, Lorraine, NSW, 28
Prest, Dorothy, NSW, 24

Redman, Patricia, Vic, 90
Reed, Margaret, NZ, 120
Richards, Mary Ellen Haggerty, USA, 126
Riley, Chris, NSW, 37
Robertson, Pamela, NZ, 121
Robertson, Patricia, Qld, 60
Robinson, Fay, NSW, back cover, 38
Robinson, Josie, SA, 108
Roche, Marjorie, NSW, 17
Rodger, Grace, NZ, 122
Rowe, Beth, NSW, 31

Sampson, Marilyn, Tas, 76
Sanders, Lee, SA, 106
Sasamoto, Nobuko, Japan, 137
Sato, Kayoko, Japan, 140
Saunders, Edie (Edith), NSW, 41
Saward, Kath (Kathleen), NZ, 122
Seager, Ruth, SA, 106
Seaman, Annette, NSW, 42
Seymour, Judy, Vic, 91
Seccombe, Jenny, NSW, 41
Shinkfield, Pauline, Vic, 92
Sievers, Betty, NZ, 112
Smith, Margaret, Vic, 92
Spencer, Arleen, Tas, 73
Spina, Carlos, Brazil, 130
Spokes, Jean, NSW, 22
Strong, Annette, NSW, 44
Stuchbery, Jean, SA, 109

Tait, Bette, Vic, 94
Takeuchi, Kae, Japan, 136
Tarry, Joyce, NSW, 45
Torkington, Barbara, ACT, 46
Towler, Margaret, NSW, 52, 53
Treacher, Moira, Vic, 94
Try, Pat, NSW, 48, 49

Uzzell, Maureen, SA, 108

Van Os, Anice, Vic, 93

Walker, Barbara, USA, 126
Walker, Gwynneth, Tas, 76
Wallace, Ena, NSW, 47
Watt, Lexie, NSW, 50, 51
Whitty, Pam, ACT, 27
Williams, Gladys (Glad), NSW, 45

Yatchman, Ruth, USA, 127